BOX BREAKERS!

The Secrets of Innovation
and Creative Thinking in Business

FREDDA McDONALD

BoxBreakers!
The Secrets of Innovation and Creative Thinking in Business

Fredda McDonald

Published by:

Paradies/Inspire LLC
P.O. Box 20393
Tampa, FL 33622
Tel: (727) 201-2585

www.paradiesinspire.com

Paradies
Publishing Company

Paradies/Inspire LLC and the Paradies/Inspire logo are registered service mark/trademark of Paradies Inspire LLC.

Printed in the United States of America

ISBN: 978-1-941102-11-4

First Edition

Copyright © 2015 Fredda McDonald. All rights reserved. No part of this publication may be reproduced, distributed, or transmitted in any form or by any means, including photocopying, recording, or other electronic or mechanical methods, without the prior written permission of the publisher, except in the case of brief quotations embodied in critical reviews and certain other noncommercial uses permitted by copyright law. For permission requests, write to the publisher, addressed "Attention: Permissions Coordinator," at the address below.

Chuck —

Thanks for inspiring the credit union industry and for always being an encourager to me!

Judy Mac
Nov. 2015

TABLE OF CONTENTS

Foreword 7
Introduction 9
Chapter One: Start with a Problem 11
Chapter Two: It's Nothing New 17
Chapter Three: Uber Evolution 29
Chapter Four: What's Prom Got to Do with It? 39
Chapter Five: Innovation on Safari 49
Chapter Six: Call the Help Desk 57
Chapter Seven: The Imperative of Innovation 63
Chapter Eight: Build Your Team. Let Your Team Build. 69
Chapter Nine: Step to the Music 77
Conclusion 101
Post Script: Street Cred. 103
Acknowledgements 107
About The Author 109
References 115

FOREWORD

Innovation is increasingly becoming the differentiator for the companies today that are surviving and thriving in our rapidly evolving global economy. And business leaders are clamoring to get ahead by finding ways to get their company "out of the box" to drive meaningful innovation.

In America, we are greatly enamored with technology and we are very proud of our heritage as a country of inventors. But how recently have we actually invented anything new? Is innovation really synonymous with newness or should it be defined in another way? And furthermore, is invention really the ticket to success or it is actually true innovation that gets us ahead?

Several imaginative companies are changing the game in traditional industries, and they are boldly challenging our thinking. But these challengers haven't really invented anything new at all. They have simply innovated and broken the box by the combination of elements that make up their solution. And technology has not been their answer in many cases, it has simply been their enabler. Often they have succeeded with technology that is readily available and has already been tested in the marketplace.

In this book, we will explore their stories in order to see the difference between invention and innovation. Additionally, we will provide insights and tools that will help you access your best ideas and assets to make a meaningful difference—regardless of the market or industry you serve.

After all, innovation is nothing new and the box can be broken.

INTRODUCTION

> *"HOUSTON, we have a problem."*
> (Apollo 13, the movie)

Anyone who has seen the movie *Apollo 13* remembers those five words vividly. On April 13, 1970, two days into their mission and just minutes after a live television update on the astronauts was sent back down to Earth, a sudden violent explosion rocked the tiny metal cylinder carrying the three astronauts through outer space. In an instant, the mission to the Moon was scrapped, and the odds of the astronauts coming home safely looked pretty slim.

It was a chilling reminder that our space program was a risky and challenging endeavor. Without the work of brilliant scientists and engineers, the thrilling missions to the Moon would never have happened in the first place. In the case of Apollo 13, as Americans sat paralyzed in front of their televisions watching a real-life drama unfold before them, everyone was counting on those brilliant minds to bring the astronauts home safely. The folks in Houston were under intense pressure, and the world was watching.

Their challenge grew exponentially when they discovered that the carbon dioxide levels in the spacecraft were climbing to very dangerous levels. At that point, it looked like getting the astronauts back to Earth needed to take a temporary backseat to just keeping them alive while they were out in space.

Houston did, indeed, have a problem.

CHAPTER ONE
START WITH A PROBLEM

> *"A problem is a chance for you to do your best."*
>
> Duke Ellington

As harsh as it sounds, a problem may not be a bad place to begin.

Often it is some kind of crisis that leads us to a new breakthrough, whether it's a shift in the market dynamics or a political or cultural upheaval. And although a crisis is not always necessary to foster innovation, problem solving absolutely is. If an idea or an invention does not fundamentally solve a problem, then it's just an idea. It is not really an innovation.

Furthermore, the speed of change has reached a velocity that is creating an unprecedented level of stress on individuals by increasing the competitive pressures in the marketplace. The interconnectedness of commerce through instant access to information around the globe has accelerated the ability of non-traditional players to disrupt traditional businesses. The advent of these new challenges is a glaring reminder that the most important currency we have to trade is truly our ideas.

However, the value of those ideas is directly related to their ultimate adoption, and that adoption has to be linked to solving a problem. There are a plethora of new business concepts and innovations that never achieve commercial success, even though they pass the "coolness" test. For instance, a Segway is a cool product, but not widely used by consumers. When the Segway was first introduced, the hype reached a fever pitch, with predictions that it would be one of the most exciting inventions since the personal computer. However, a decade later, these vehicles are still considered a novelty. There may be a number of reasons why

Segway did not achieve mass commercial success, but *not* solving a problem was certainly one of them.

To truly fit the definition of "meaningful innovation" a business idea must first address a need, improve a process, increase productivity, or make life easier. Sometimes the problem is an obvious one, but oftentimes it's not. Sometimes, it is a problem that is created from a crisis, such as the one that faced the NASA engineers on April 13, 1970.

Because of the explosion, the astronauts were forced to move out of the command module into the Lunar Excursion Module (LEM), which was still attached and ready to be deployed. Moving them into the LEM was logical and seemed like a brilliant idea because it was fully equipped to support life. However, it wasn't built to support life for very long. The air filtration system was only designed with enough capability to take two astronauts down to the Moon and bring them back to the command module. Slowly but surely, as Commander Jim Lovell and astronauts Fred Haise and Jack Swigert were jammed into the LEM together and time was ticking by, the carbon dioxide levels were rising and the team at Mission Control in Houston began breathing heavily.

The first solution they considered was simply to take the carbon dioxide scrubbers out of the command module and replace the ones that were failing in the LEM. However, because the filters for the command module were square, they would not fit into the round cartridge for the LEM. The problem presented itself simply because no one at NASA had the foresight to see that the filters should be designed to be interoperable.

So they gathered the experts on hand at Mission Control, dumped all of the available materials in the LEM and the Command Module out on a table, and took a good, long look. The items on the table were obviously all they had to work with because there was no way to send anything else up to the spacecraft. Meanwhile, oxygen and time were both running out.

It was under these conditions and constraints that the engineers improvised a solution that is still known fondly at NASA as the "Square Peg in the Round Hole." The Rube Goldberg-type solution involved taking an oxygen hose from one of the lunar landing suits and connecting that hose to the Command Module square canister filter with duct tape. Luckily, duct tape was loaded on board every mission. The engineers may not have appreciated the need for interoperability of parts, but they clearly understood the necessity of adding duct tape to the ship's manifest. The seal that it provided enabled them to use the suit's fan to draw carbon dioxide from the cabin through the canister and send it back into the LEM as oxygen. They tried it out in the simulator, and it worked.

Working in the simulator in Houston was one thing, but they also had to engineer it in such a way that the astronauts could put the pieces together easily and quickly by themselves in space. Even as the contraption was being designed and configured, the engineers had a focused goal in front of them—make it easy. They wrote down the assembly instructions as they built it and then walked the astronauts through construction of the device verbally over the radio.

Thankfully, that problem was solved; everyone literally began to breathe easy and the full focus of the team in Houston was turned back to the mission of bringing the astronauts home. But the meaningful innovation which emerged to benefit future projects, both inside and outside of NASA, was the adoption of interoperability as a key component of future design. That insight has now become a mantra for engineers in many industries, making manufacturing more productive and economical.

There are many other important lessons that can be drawn from the Apollo 13 incident by looking at exactly how the team at NASA responded to the crisis. Far from being just an interesting retrospective, these lessons can drive meaningful innovation in your business today.

For starters, the limited resources of the team were both a constraint and an asset. The one thing that the team in Houston knew for sure was that the only available materials they could use were currently in the hands of the astronauts. Interestingly, that limitation, along with a time constraint that spelled life or death, was actually a driver for their creativity. It focused their energy by limiting their possibilities.

You may not be facing life-and-death problems in your business today, but you can still drive innovation *by starting with what you have* as a powerful and enabling business principle when approaching challenges. It does not matter if you are running a dress shop or driving a limo—the principle is the same. As we will see, both of these traditional industries are being disrupted today.

CHAPTER TWO
IT'S NOTHING NEW

> *"There is no new thing under the sun."*
> Ecclesiastes 1:9, King James Version

Consumers are constantly clamoring for the next new thing, and a great many extraordinary products have come into the marketplace in the past decade, such as smart phones and tablet devices. American consumers are particularly enamored with things that are new, and geeks will camp out at Apple stores for days to be the first to get their hands on the latest and greatest. As the early adopters of technology, Americans drive more than our fair share of global consumption, in large part because of our love affair with newness. It is easy to take a quantum leap from there and think that *innovation* equals *a new invention,* but that is just not true.

Often the innovations that change our lives the most are really things that have been with us for some time. Just like the engineering team on the Apollo 13 mission found out, our resources are there in front of us—they just haven't been dumped on the table and put together in a uniquely functioning way before. It could be because a crisis has not occurred to prompt us to look at them differently.

One way to think about this as a business principle is to consider for a moment the powerful concept of *ecology* in innovation. *Merriam-Webster* defines ecology as "a branch of science concerned with the interrelationship of organisms and their environments." We have come to realize that as a society we must focus on protecting our natural environment; this means the careful utilization of our existing resources, so when we say something is *ecological,* we likely mean it is a wise use of resources.

The realization that our planet needs to be carefully protected has become a vital issue that is at the top of the agenda when international leaders get together to talk about priorities. Additionally, most of us interact with our environment in a more responsible way by recycling our cans and bottles and taking our own shopping bag to the grocery store. As a result, we are finding increasingly better ways to manage our interrelationship with our planet than we have in the past.

Ironically, when we look at the problems we have to solve in our business, we often miss the opportunity to use that very same principle. The premise of this, called the Ecology Principle, is that we should look at our business ecosystem in the same way we look at our natural ecosystem—by paying attention to the interrelationship of our assets and thinking about utilizing what we have in a better way instead of creating something new. We need to take a phrase from Apple's advertising in 1997 that drove English teachers crazy and "Think Different" if we are to embark on the innovation path.

Many business people are familiar with the tools and processes used by consultants to address business issues. Asset Theory has long been a driver of problem solving in business, and it is at the core of the venerable SWOT analysis, so often used. Carefully examining Strengths, Weaknesses, Opportunities and Threats can lead to breakthrough insights and novel solutions to business problems. So when consultants bring out the SWOT grid, what is the first question they ask a client? "What are your strengths?" This sets teams off to brainstorm about the obvious assets of the organization.

When we think of innovation, we usually start by looking for something brand new. But as the SWOT demonstrates, there is a proven fundamental power in starting the process of analyzing solutions by looking first at what you have. However, the SWOT process can overlook hidden assets or underutilized assets, which may be the most meaningful ones when it comes to opportunities for innovation. And the SWOT analysis does not lend itself to finding combinations of existing assets with other things that may be readily available in the marketplace.

Conversely, the Ecology Principle begins with the theory that something right under your nose may be the best enabler of your next innovation. Putting things together in a new way could be the secret to success. As an example, let's explore an innovation from the 1950s that had a lasting impact on our culture today. The following is a story about how train cars full of frozen turkeys collided with the phenomenon of television viewing.

During that decade, American families became obsessed with television. Harkening back to the *Merriam-Webster* definition of ecology, people were most definitely interacting differently with their ecosystem. They were sitting around together every night in front of what we would now consider a very tiny black-and-white television screen. This became the nightly pastime of millions of families. With only three networks on the dial (yes, it was a dial), they watched favorite weekly television programs and happily consumed a limited choice of entertainment on the schedule that was offered up to them. More plainly stated, there was not much to choose from, and they couldn't even decide when they wanted to watch it. And they happily did this together almost every night.

Contrast that with our situation today—thousands of channels available and the ability to select programs "on demand" to be viewed on very large televisions at home with high-density details or laptop computers on the go. We have screens of all sizes—from big screens to tiny tablets—endless choices in entertainment, and mobile access whenever we want it. Interestingly, our consumption of entertainment is a more solitary endeavor than ever—television is rarely watched together as a family.

However, in the '50s and '60s, long-running series such as *Gunsmoke*, *Leave It To Beaver*, and *The Ed Sullivan Show* were watched by multiple generations all sitting together in the same room. This was a sociological phenomenon that fundamentally rewove the fiber of American society. As archaic as this scenario sounds today, television was a technological breakthrough that changed everything in our cultural ecosystem. Not only would the advertising and entertainment industries never be the same, neither would the interpersonal dynamic of families, thanks to television.

This major shift in the tectonic plates of family social interaction coincidentally collided with an otherwise unrelated occurrence: the overproduction of turkeys. Robert Klara wrote a fascinating article in *Adweek* about how these two seemingly unrelated events changed our culture. In 1954, the team at C.A. Swanson & Sons over-projected the demand for turkeys and found themselves with railcars full of unmarketable frozen fowl. This dilemma came with the unfortunate wrinkle that the only way the refrigerator system worked on the trains was to keep them moving. Consequently, Swanson had trains traveling back and forth across the country full of frozen turkeys until the company could find a solution. However, thanks to innovative thinking, those chilly railcars soon turned into hot gravy trains.

According to Klara's article, a resourceful member of Swanson's sales team had recently traveled on American Airlines, and he gained inspiration from the metal tray with compartments the flight attendants used to serve his meal. He suggested to Swanson that they create a whole meal around the frozen turkey and provide it to consumers in a metal tray that could be heated in the oven. Here was the big "ah ha": they could call the frozen meal a "TV dinner" because it was to be served while the family was gathered around the television set. The team researched meal ingredients that could be frozen and heated together concurrently with turkey—such as cornbread stuffing, sweet potatoes, green peas, and, of course, gravy—and the TV dinner was born. The company sold 25 million of them before the end of the year, according to the *Adweek* article. Since we have been referencing it previously.

The article also highlights how brilliant the marketing angle was because it appealed to the desire for mothers to provide a well-balanced meal they could easily prepare and the family could eat together in front of the television. But to highlight the Ecology Principle, as we saw with Apollo 13, the solution was born out of an emergency situation solved by the team using a unique combination of existing and familiar assets.

In today's world, the frozen meal section at the supermarket consumes a whole aisle, and there is barely a freezer in America that doesn't have some modern variation of that original TV dinner in it. But at its origin, this innovation and subsequent iterations really were born out of the Ecology Principle.

Both the Swanson team and the NASA team were presented with an immediate challenge, and they started looking around at familiar assets on hand in order to solve it. The common denominator in both cases was that the "boots on the ground" people found a solution by creating an imaginative combination of existing and familiar assets. Just as we often overlook the power of our assets, we overlook the power of our people, too.

Secondly, the fix the Swanson product developers were seeking had to be *easy for consumers*. Just as the Houston engineers were challenged to create a solution the astronauts could assemble easily, the Swanson team had to create a meal that could be prepared and served quickly and easily.

As context, the families of the '50s and '60s felt they had become very busy, so they were more tuned in to products that were convenient. Innovations such as cake mix, instant pudding, and paper towels had come along to give the modern family more time. The idea that these frozen meals could be quickly heated in the oven all at once was a vital feature. (This was before microwave ovens, too.) So thanks to Swanson TV dinners, the very busy American family had more quality time to sit down and watch *Leave It to Beaver* together. Just think of the impact on the Baby Boomer generation.

Finally, it was important that the folks at Swanson were *economical* in their solution. Those turkeys would not keep, and there was only so long they could travel around the country in railcars. The clock was ticking, resources were limited, and time was of the essence. Even with those constraints, the Swanson team knew they had to create a final product that would appeal to the budget-conscious family. Economic necessity is still an essential factor in meaningful innovation today. Widespread adoption is always predicated on solutions that are *economical*. Regardless of the appeal of an innovation, it will not get traction if it is too expensive, and nothing is more *economical* than using what you already have.

Here is a personal example I learned from nature. Several years ago, I built an outdoor shower at a little cottage I own at the beach. I originally added it on to be able to wash the sand off my big dog and brush out the fur in his soft, downy undercoat, which seemed to constantly shed when we were at the beach. Since I built the shower with tall privacy walls and a hot water hookup, it also became a morning tradition for me to shower outdoors when I stayed at the cottage. The fresh morning air combined with the sights and sounds of nature at that time of day were always invigorating.

    One spring morning, while enjoying my outdoor shower, I got to watch a mother bird who decided to build her nest in the limb of a tree that hung overhead. She was meticulous in her construction, and it was fascinating to watch her bring little twigs to weave together as a place to lay her eggs. I watched her for several days, and then one morning, when she came in for a landing with a twig in her beak, I saw a little poof of fur flying in her nest. She took off again and came back a few minutes later with a beak full of matted fur in her mouth. I realized she was picking up the fur I brushed off my dog to line her nest. That was very resourceful of Mama Bird, and also very insightful for us. Just like the engineers at NASA and the Swanson product designers, the bird used the resources she found readily available.

Combined with the Ecology Principle, we can add two more "E's" to our innovation framework: *Economical* and *Easy*. To that end, here are questions to consider:

How powerful might it be to proactively unleash the resources we already have rather than expending vast amounts of energy looking for something new?

What are we missing by not looking in our own backyard?

What if the simplicity of familiarity has an unrecognized power to unleash innovation?

Furthermore, what if tapping into the brain trust of the people closest to our products and most familiar with our underutilized assets and focusing them on making the final use case *easy* and *economical* unleashes their talents to roam on a great new frontier for disruption and innovation?

Let's explore some practical examples of recent use cases that demonstrate the Principle of The Three E's: Ecological, Economical and Easy in practice. These examples will help you see how you can take the insights from unlikely places like the Apollo 13 crisis, the Swanson TV dinners, and the practical Mama Bird to proactively "break the box" within your own company and gain real traction, regardless of your business.

CHAPTER THREE

UBER EVOLUTION

> *"If you think you can do a thing or think you can't do a thing, you are right."*
>
> — *Henry Ford*

Henry Ford forever changed the landscape of our planet by creating an inexpensive way to produce automobiles, making them accessible to the common person. We now have a world where individual ownership of a vehicle seems to be an inalienable right in many cultures around the globe. In spite of the negative impact of pollution and the relentless demand for fossil fuel that comes along with cars, people want to own them, and they feel entitled to the independence automobiles provide to them.

Many people credit Henry Ford with inventing the car, but even though Ford brought automobiles to the masses, he did not actually invent the automobile. Twenty-two years before Ford began to manufacture the Model T, a German inventor named Karl Benz patented the Benz Patent-Motorwagen, which was the first commercially produced gasoline-powered "horseless carriage." Even prior to Benz's invention, there were several iterations of motorized vehicles that used other forms of combustion.

However, the innovative mind of Ford took the basic invention and turned it into a product that could be rapidly adopted because it was affordable to the masses. By creating the assembly line and standardizing the product, thus making it *economical* to produce, he was successful in bringing the automobile into the mainstream. As part of the streamlined production, he was famously quoted as saying a consumer could get a Model T in any color, "so long as it is black." Limiting options was pivotal to making the car affordable, as well.

One fact that many people are not aware of is that cars, which are created to move us from place to place, sit parked 95% of the time. It is surprising, but it is true. Automobiles are an over-proliferated and extremely underutilized resource. They are actually not being used for the purpose they were created for the vast majority of the time; they are just taking up space in parking lots and garages.

The underutilization of the automobile is the very thing that makes the transportation industry ripe for disruption today—and being disrupted it is. Even more to the point, the new disrupters in this ecosystem are taking better advantage of the underutilized assets. And the taxi cab industry is feeling it the most.

Just a few years ago, city dwellers often lamented the necessity of taking a cab. It was hard to find one when you needed it, especially during bad weather and rush hour. Taxi drivers were notorious for being rude, and the cabs they drove were sometimes dirty. The drivers usually wanted to take cash, and often the riders found they were fresh out of cash once they hailed a cab. The iconic pretty girl all dressed up for the evening standing on the curb to hail a cab only to get splashed by an inconsiderate taxi driver careening over a mud puddle was a favorite scene of movie directors. The same was true of the proverbial fight over who hailed the taxi first as two riders slide into the same back seat. Altogether, taxicabs have been the prototypical bad consumer experience, second only to actually buying a car, which always ranks at the top of everyone's list. So far, nothing about the interrelationships within this ecosystem of transportation sounds like much fun.

The exception to this scenario was riding in a limousine, the regular means of transportation for mostly the wealthy or famous. Business people on expense accounts hired limousines, and parents of lucky prom-goers rented stretch limos for their kids on that special occasion. However, it was rare for most consumers to hire a limo.

Very few limousine drivers made a lot of money because they were underutilized. They didn't spend much time actually driving because few people could afford them as a regular means of transportation. That very dynamic meant their hourly rate had to be high enough to cover all the time they sat parked, listening to music and contemplating how they could write the next great American novel. Other than missing out on winning that Pulitzer Prize, the major complaint of many limo drivers was that dispatchers played favorites, making it difficult to fill out a full shift with riders. It was an economic dilemma that kept rates high and utilization low.

So how did the underutilization of luxury transportation finally collide with the dissatisfying experience of riding in a taxi? It's called Uber—the highly celebrated mobile app that connects riders and drivers. It emerged because the ecosystem was ripe for it. The formula is this: underutilized assets plus a bad consumer experience equal a perfect opportunity for disruption.

Uber first rolled out its solution in San Francisco in 2010 with independent limo drivers who were primarily recruited through social media. Through the same means, word got out to consumers that the misery of the taxicab experience was over. "Uber" tranlated into "problem solved" for San Francisco and then for cities around the world—and today Uber is in 58 countries and is still expanding.

The launch of this game-changing mobile app connecting people with a limousine at a discount price allowed consumers to access a luxury ride whenever they wanted. There was no more standing on a street corner hoping to find an available passing taxi; the frustrated riders and the underutilized drivers could easily ride in style via the magic of technology.

The technology that supports the Uber innovation is really fascinating in its simplicity. For the consumer, once the app is downloaded, all of the available cars nearby appear on the screen of the mobile device, along with the estimated time it will take the closest driver to arrive. It is just as *easy* as pushing a button to call a car to the consumer's location, which is determined by the geo-locator on the phone. The payment method is a preloaded debit or credit card. Riders no longer fumble around with their wallets when they reach their destinations because the payment is already complete. The best news? The limo is basically the same price of a taxicab—sometimes less.

The good folks at Uber didn't stop their innovating there, because the transportation ecosystem has more underutilized resources than just limo drivers. Remember all of those parked cars in garages and driveways belonging to consumers? Once Uber perfected the solution for limos, the next thing launched was an app that allows the consumer to call an "UberX." It's not a limo, it's just a very nice car owned by an average individual who may also be an aspiring novelist. Suddenly, those garages and parking lots full of idle and underutilized cars began to be utilized! With this expansion, not only limo drivers are profiting from providing transportation, so are lots of other people who want to use their personal cars to make money in their spare time.

Uber's success has given rise to other new companies, like Lyft and SideCar, who utilize this same technology of mobile apps, geo-locators, and embedded payments to take advantage of this underutilized asset of parked cars. Lyft is the company in San Francisco that added the fanciful component of a big pink mustache that drivers attach to the front of their cars to identify them as Lyft drivers. The company is also known for its drivers' creativity with snacks, soft drinks, and magazines for the riders to enjoy as well. They took the same concept as Uber and made it more fun.

Additionally, taxi companies in many cities are now adopting the geo-locator technology that Uber uses and providing payment apps to consumers so that they are able to connect and easily pay for a cab. The impact of these transportation innovations has been felt around the world and throughout the entire industry.

To dissect how it happened, let's examine the question, "What exactly did Uber invent?" If you take a look at the pieces and parts of Uber, you have to say, not much new, really. The geo-locator technology that connects the rider to the car is not new. The payment protocol in the app was not Uber's invention; it was already in the market. Furthermore, Uber does not directly employ drivers, nor does it own fleets of cars, maintenance facilities, or fuel stations.

Uber simply linked all of these things together in the same way the engineers at Mission Control used the hose from the lunar landing suit and matched it up with the canister from the LEM—by using existing resources. Uber put existing resources together in a unique way to improve the transportation ecosystem. The use case for an improved consumer experience bears out the principles of the 3 E's perfectly. If you build it, they will come, but only if it is *economical*, you make it *easy*, and you utilize the existing resources of the *ecosystem* wisely.

In the case of Uber, it is also important to take note that they not only disrupted individual transportation—all forms of ground transportation are now feeling a shift. This shift is impacting mass transit, commercial transit, and even the rental car industry with the emergence of companies like ZipCar, where rental cars are kept in unattended lots and accessed through a membership card. And Uber's latest iteration is to provide you with an opportunity to carpool with people in your area going in the same direction.

Because of Uber's dramatic success, the company is now facing great resistance from the traditional players in the transportation industry. Taxi drivers have rioted, legislators have tried to write laws to prevent Uber from entering certain markets, and attorneys have found ways to sue. However, innovation cannot be legislated away, and the bell of disruption can not be unrung. Uber as a company may change, evolve, or morph into something else, but transportation will never return to the pre-Uber status quo.

Cars sitting idle 95% of the time were the signal that disruption was on the way. And Uber is only the beginning. Just imagine where transportation will go tomorrow. The combination of driverless cars and Uber technology presents a scenario that promises to disrupt and evolve transportation in ways that are hard for us to comprehend. Car ownership may become a thing of the past as we pull up our app and call a driverless car to our doorstep. That would certainly be *easy, economical,* and absolutely *ecological.*

Any industry sitting on excess capacity—possibly your industry—should be on alert. Because here is the most important lesson of all: *idle capacity in any form makes your company a sitting duck, simply waiting for disruption.*

CHAPTER FOUR

WHAT'S PROM GOT TO DO WITH IT?

> *"Prom has all the elements of a popular story. It reeks of all-Americanness … It has romance. Pretty dresses. Dancing. Limos. High School. Coming of age."*
>
> — Adora Svitak, Author, Age 17

T he evolution of the high school prom into a socially defining life experience has proven to be quite expensive for parents in the past few years. As we noted previously, some lucky prom-goers have parents who foot the bill for a limo, and those teens in the stretch ride get kicked up a notch higher on the high school coolness-rating indicator. In addition to the cost of the limo, a big impact on the budget for the families of those high school kids is the high fashion. Guys have to rent a tuxedo, and those pretty prom dresses for the girls are not cheap.

Unfortunately, the prom dress can only be worn once because teenage girls absolutely, positively, and under no circumstance will have their picture taken wearing the same dress that they wore last year, especially since the advent of social media. Those prom pictures will live on Facebook forever. To quote any red-blooded teenage American girl when asked what would happen if she wore her prom dress twice, "I would just die." Author Adora Svitak is quite right—prom does have all of the dramatic elements of a popular story.

For girls who go on to college and join a sorority, this expensive situation gets even worse because there are two formals a year—a fall and a spring formal. Considering the repeat group of sorority sisters and fraternity brothers at those events, fashion simply demands a new dress. After four years of that—you can do the math. It amounts to eight once-worn dresses hanging forlornly in a closet somewhere. The prom glory has faded, and these dresses are just awaiting their fate in a thrift store collection bin. It is a sad and expensive tale, but given the Ecology Principle associated with excess and underutilized resources, it also sounds like a perfect opportunity for disruptive innovation. Leave it to some really smart women at Harvard to figure that out.

Jennifer Hyman, an MBA student at Harvard Business School, recognized this as an opportunity after witnessing her sister spending money on a new designer dress to wear to a wedding despite already owning several designer dresses. Jennifer is a very practical person, and she asked her sister why she would not wear a dress she already owned. The answer her sister gave was simple: her photo in those dresses had been posted to social media, and her Facebook friends were coming to the wedding. Hyman discussed this situation with her classmate, Jenny Fleiss, and it inspired them with a business idea for an *economical* way to wear an expensive designer dress just once by doing the same thing the guys do with their tuxes—renting them.

The more they talked through the business implications of their concept, the more they believed it had potential, so they decided to test it out with sorority girls. They bought a batch of designer dresses, drove them to a nearby college campus on formal week, and rented them out—it was a raging success. Since their concept worked beautifully, they came back to Harvard to put together a complete business plan. The Jennifers recognized that scaling the concept would require sophisticated logistical support for things like dry cleaning and tailoring repairs. They also thought through the supply chain details and determined how much money they would need to launch their business. Once their business plan was complete, they took it to the place they felt it would resonate most strongly: the fashion industry.

Through considerable moxie and great resourcefulness, these two graduate students were able to secure a meeting with one of the icons of the fashion world, Diane Von Furstenberg. They confidently explained their business plan to her and demonstrated their success with the experiment on the neighboring college campus. Much to their surprise, Ms. Von Furstenberg unceremoniously burst their bubble.

She explained that their business would not be a success because designers had no desire to have their dresses worn more than once. She pointed out that the problem they were solving for consumers drove a great deal of profitability in the fashion industry. Underutilized assets, in this case those lonely formal dresses hanging in the closet, were very valuable to her industry, because that behavior on the part of consumers helped them sell more dresses. However, just as we saw in the disruption of transportation that was created by Uber, those underutilized dresses were the very seeds of innovation. And this was an innovation that could not be stopped—not even by the mighty Diane Von Furstenberg.

Very fortunately, Ms. Hyman and Ms. Fleiss were not easily deterred. On the contrary, they recognized that the feedback from the fashion world only reinforced *why* they should move ahead. The response they got indicated to them that they had a good business plan; they had just taken the concept to the wrong funding source. So they reworked their plan to appeal to investors with more of a venture capital approach, and they were successful in getting the first round funding they needed. With that, their company, Rent the Runway, was born.

Today, the company does over $100 million in annual revenue, and it is growing steadily. This is an incredible accomplishment for two young women who haven't turned thirty yet. Ironically, they rent quite a few Diane Von Furstenberg dresses, and she is very glad they do.

This is how they do it.

They developed an easy-to-use website with online ordering so average consumers can quickly search for just the right dress for that special occasion. Rent the Runway (RTR) also employs highly trained and helpful customer service representatives in their call center to answer questions for consumers about how the dresses fit and to advise the women before they rent. RTR will automatically send two sizes with each order, just in case there is a question about what the right size would be for a given individual. RTR also offers a discount if the consumer wants to order a second dress as back up, and that back up dress is sent in two sizes as well.

In addition to the professional models who are pictured on the website, consumers can post candid shots of themselves wearing the dress. Therefore customers can see the dress on women of all sizes, not just pencil-thin models. Very importantly, these consumers write recommendations on the website about their own experience after wearing the dress, including information on the fit, the length, and the most vital information of all, how it made them *feel*. One of the things their early research revealed was that women made fashion choices because of how it made them feel, not how it made them look. It was an important distinction—one that is lost on some companies in the fashion industry. This data caused RTR to be very careful in designing its total consumer experience to maximize that good feeling.

One of the hurdles of the rental experience the founders also anticipated was the consumers' fear of damaging expensive gowns. The solution is that RTR insures all of the clothes, so if there is a mishap of a torn hem or spilled wine, the consumer does not bear the liability. Under the banner of making it *easy*, the packaging for shipping the dresses back to RTR is pre-labeled and included with the dress when it is delivered. Rent the Runway also takes care of dry cleaning the dress upon its return. Once it's been worn, the consumer simply stuffs the dress in a pre-labeled bag and has UPS pick it up. A designer formal might sell for $2,500 retail, and it usually comes to the consumer signed, sealed, and delivered from RTR for around $150. This is more than just a story of economy and consumer satisfaction; it is also a story about big data analytics.

This company that was once snubbed by high-end designers has now "broken the box" of the fashion industry by using predictive analytics to determine the inventory buy. RTR analyzes trends, regionally, by age and by fashion event category; they know the difference in fashion trends between a prom, a wedding, or a charity gala. There is also a regional difference in taste between Memphis and Manhattan. RTR is applying this scientific approach with analytics to understand what women want to wear, because they recognized early on that it was an expensive and logistical nightmare to guess.

Their data analysts can predict which dresses Southern women wear to weddings versus what women in the Pacific Northwest want to wear to the annual country club formal. They can tell you the color trends for teenagers at prom in Charleston versus what thirty somethings wear in California out for a special night on the town. And thankfully, they know ahead of time when that ever-popular mermaid skirt for formals is finally going to be swimming away as a fashion trend.

The team at RTR is not just using this data to drive their fashion buy; they are now taking their findings and influencing designers. By using big data, Rent the Runway is actually impacting which dresses make it to the runway and also onto retail racks. With over 4 million members in its database, the company is a serious force to be reckoned with in fashion. In a short period of time, the Jennifers have come a long way from just being two graduate students with a well-executed power point. They are now industry drivers.

As successful as they are, what did they actually invent?

Again, just as we saw when we took a look at Uber, not really very much. Online ordering had been around for quite a while when they launched their website. They took advantage of retail search engines, but they didn't create a new one. The logistics involved in managing, shipping, and turning their inventory around are part of supply chain science that has been in place for many years. They hired experienced logistics professionals to create a vertically integrated environment so that they are not dependent on outside vendors such as dry cleaners.

Even though they are influencers of fashion, they do not employ designers, nor do they manufacture dresses. They simply sell the dresses the designers produce. Lastly, they certainly did not invent big data, but they have taken its use to a new level in fashion by determining what dresses they offer and how they can leverage their data to negotiate with fashion designers.

By applying online ordering, supply chain logistics, and data analytics to their fashion buy and inventory management in a unique way, they created meaningful innovation, which is being widely and enthusiastically adopted. They didn't invent anything, however, so it is The Ecology Principle at its best. What they really did was link together existing technology and processes to create a solution that helps women access the fashion ecosystem in a more responsible way by better utilizing an underutilized resource.

Looking through the filter of the Principle of the 3 E's, Rent the Runway is absolutely *ecological*, it is certainly *easy* to use, and it is radically *economical*.

CHAPTER FIVE

INNOVATION ON SAFARI

> *"Living on $6 a day means you have a refrigerator, a TV, a cell phone, your children can go to school. That's not possible on $1 a day."*
>
> Bill Gates

Eight years ago, the economy in Kenya was in trouble. Its currency had failed, and the conditions, both politically and socially, in the country were in great decline, potentially on the verge of chaos. Today that is not the case. Kenya enjoys one of the strongest economies and most stable political environments in Africa, and the turnaround may be due to the *ecological* use of old mobile devices and refurbished feature phones with a new all-digital currency called M-Pesa.

Pesa is the Swahili word for money, and in 2007, the largest mobile network operators in Kenya and Tanzania got together to launch a mobile phone-based payment service they named M-Pesa. The fundamental idea was to use mobile devices and the value that had become associated with airtime, which was already being bartered, as a currency that would replace cash. The service allowed consumers to pay for goods, as well as deposit, transfer, and withdraw money, using text messaging on a mobile device with the M-Pesa digital currency. The adoption of this currency type was enhanced because it used retail outlets, instead of just banks, as its network for access and distribution. Additionally, the mobile network operators made it affordable by offering a refurbished "feature phone" device for free to consumers who could not afford one.

Now almost 17 million people in Kenya are registered users of this service. It has essentially replaced cash as the primary means of transacting commerce there. And, interestingly enough, it has also reduced the crimes associated with cash and made the country safer. The Bill and Melinda Gates

Foundation has been instrumental in providing funding to support this program, along with other altruistic endeavors in developing countries. Even so, it is really the ingenuity of the government regulators working together with the mobile network operators and financial institutions that have made it a widespread success. In fact, people are going to Kenya from all over the world to learn how to make mobile payments more successful in more developed countries.

In the US we consider ourselves a very advanced nation, but mobile payments have only recently become mainstream in the United States with the introduction of Apple Pay and now Android Pay. But compared to Kenya, we may not be all that advanced when it comes to mobile payments. Some of the original advancements in payments in the US, such as credit cards with magnetic stripes, have actually set us back in terms of mobile technology. This is due in part to the expensive point-of-sale systems used by US merchants that are all based on magnetic stripe technology.

However, this old technology actually slowed the adoption of mobile payments since expensive new POS technology was required at checkout to allow retailers to accept payments from phones. On the contrary, in Kenya, cash was the major form of commerce at the time things were crashing down. When M-Pesa was introduced, there was no hurdle of a magnetic stripe at checkout. In fact, merchants who wanted to participate in M-Pesa simply needed to get a cellular phone to receive payment. It is very simple and *easy* for consumers and merchants alike because the payments are easily enabled via text on the most rudimentary of mobile devices.

You probably thought your old Blackberry or iPhone had ended up in a landfill somewhere. *Au contraire*, it may be out on the plains of Tanzania right now, enabling an African farmer to buy seeds. Or, it may be in the hands of a woman in Nairobi, enabling her to transact business at her roadside fruit stand. In addition to reducing crime in a society that had been mostly cash based, the advent of the M-Pesa also enabled many women to fully participate in the economy for the first time. Until M-Pesa came along, there were still many tribes in Kenya that did not allow women to touch money. This rule was an incredibly effective way to shut women out of the economy and simultaneously rob them of their social power. However, the tribal rulers who forbade touching money had never considered the possibility that money could become digital; no tribal rules mandate that women not touch mobile devices.

One story that is particularly heartwarming and demonstrates just how life changing this innovation has been relates to a woman from Kenya I met several years ago, we will call Ester. She had five children, and she had never worked outside the home. Unfortunately, even though her husband had a job, he spent a lot of his money on banana beer. This left Ester in the unenviable position of having to scrape and struggle to hold her home and family together without being able to touch money.

When M-Pesa emerged, Ester had a great business idea. She took her plan to a local credit union and asked if she could open an account for her new business. They agreed to let her join the credit union and also gave her advice and counsel on starting her new venture since she had never been in business before. She was determined to make it work and was sure her idea was a good one. The happy ending to this story is that today Ester is very successful, and she also employs two of her sons in her company. Her business concept? She manufactures banana beer.

Ester is not alone in her successful venture. Many women in Kenya are incredibly entrepreneurial, and they are taking advantage of mobile payments to become vital contributors to the economy. They are starting small businesses in record numbers, creating micro-lending schemes, and demonstrating how impactful a group of empowered women can be in turning economic woes into economic energy. Ironically enough, this movement was actually facilitated by the lack of existing technology in the form of magnetic stripe card payments; thus, that step could be bypassed. Kenya was essentially a blank slate for payments innovation, but the key elements of success already existed: a national mobile network operator and the technology that enabled money movement via text message. Nothing new had to be invented.

One of the most vital factors for success of the M-Pesa mobile payments system is that it is *easy* for consumers. Adoption has been rapid and widespread because using these mobile devices is so intuitive. M-Pesa also demonstrates the Ecology Principle in every sense. By taking advantage of previously reused and refurbished mobile devices, this innovation is taking advantage of existing resources. Furthermore, by utilizing existing retail establishments for cash back and deposit services, the M-Pesa currency system takes maximum advantage of what is already there.

Lastly, this innovation took off because it is very *economical.* Under the circumstances that M-Pesa was introduced in Kenya, it would have been impossible to get widespread adoption without extremely *economical* delivery. The devices themselves are provided for free or at a very nominal cost because the mobile network operator ultimately gains revenue from the airtime utilization. M-Pesa is a real box breaker, because the financial lives of the consumers of Kenya are steadily improving as they become mainstreamed into traditional relationships with financial institutions, and they are creating thriving businesses as the economy of the country improves.

In the country of Kenya, which most Americans would consider undeveloped, millions of people are transacting in one of the most highly digitized economies on earth. Kenya is brilliantly demonstrating the Principle of the 3 E's in action.

CHAPTER SIX
CALL THE HELP DESK

> *"We cannot teach people anything; we can only help them discover it within themselves."*
>
> *Galileo Galilei*

Innovation is not always about technology; technology is often just the enabler of innovation. A great example this recently happened, quite imaginatively, in India.

India has had a long and rocky road to economic stability to gain its current position of world leadership over the past century. Famously led to independence from Great Britain in 1947 by the nonviolent civil disobedience of Mahatma Gandhi, over the past decade India has become poised as a technology center of excellence. Many of America's largest corporations have outsourced domestic development and call center services to state-of-the-art facilities in cities like Bangalore, Hyderabad, and Chennai. Most people recognize the Indian accent on the other end of the line when they have trouble with their computers and call in for help desk support. However, the country of India today is not just about outsourced technology services, it has become vastly different in almost every way than it was just a decade ago.

Over 1 billion people live in India today, versus the 300 million who live in America. It is also the world's fastest-expanding economy, and Prime Minister Narendra Modi has intentions of bringing more jobs, new industries, and international prominence to his country. Modi's goal is not an easy feat because the stress upon the infrastructure of the country to support the large population is sizable, and the need to provide quality education is also one of the greatest challenges in many regions of India.

For a great many of the schoolchildren in those rural areas, the things that you would expect them to have are simply not available, including necessities like a school desk. As a consequence for many of these children, they are forced sit on the floor with their back hunched over their books to do their schoolwork. As unfortunate as this situation is, they also have the additional hardship of hauling their heavy schoolbooks for what is often a very long walk from home to school and then back again. The families of these children greatly value and support the opportunity for them to be educated, but they are not able to afford a school bag and certainly cannot fund the purchase of a school desk themselves.

At first blush, the solution to this problem might seem to be solved by reaching out to a school desk or book bag manufacturer. Surely, with the philanthropic nature of many companies, they could be asked to donate or provide these basics as an act of generosity to the children of India. The problem is that we are talking about a lot of desks and school bags. Remember those one billion people? Many of them are schoolchildren, and that is a heavy donation, even for a philanthropic company.

A second alternative would be to find a way to repurpose old desks and book bags from other places and send them to the rural areas of India.

This is not a bad idea, but it would be a logistic nightmare to gather them up and distribute them. Both of these ideas were probably explored and discussed at length by the school officials. Logic also probably led schools to reach out to other charitable organizations to provide desks and book bags. However, with millions of children in need and the logistics of delivering these desks and book bags being so difficult in these remote areas, it is just not easy.

Of course, if you are truly thinking like an *ecological* innovator and investigating a resource that is in great supply and is also underutilized would you ever think about discarded shipping boxes as the answer?

That is exactly what Aarambh did.

Aarambh is an NGO (non-government organization) that was created as a community service center for marginalized families in urban slum and rural areas in India. The organizers wanted to support underprivileged students with basic necessities in order to help them be more successful in school and take better advantage of their education. They saw instantly that there were two problems that needed immediate attention: one was the desk and the other was the school bag. Quite ingeniously they found a way to solve for both problems at once by utilizing a resource that was readily available to them: used cardboard boxes.

They created a stencil design to cut these boxes in such a way that when they were folded, they formed a school bag to carry books and when the child arrived at school, he or she could unfold the book bag to become a desk! This invention is called the Help Desk, and they are now being used effectively in remote regions to improve the quality of education for many schoolchildren.

A discarded box that was destined for the landfill is now both a desk and a book bag. *Ecological?* Yes, and it fits the use case profile of meaningful innovation theory perfectly. These boxes are also *economical,* costing less than 20 cents each to manufacture. Now the families of millions of school children are in reach of both a desk and a book bag at that price. Assembly is also incredibly *easy.* The kids can quickly transform their bag into a desk and at the end of the day reverse the process to carry their books home.

The students now have a much richer educational experience, which will give them a better chance to be successful in life. This is meaningful innovation at its best, and thanks to a resourceful group at Aarambh, this box breaker perfectly expresses the power of the 3 E's—it's *economical, easy,* and *ecological.*

It also gives the Help Desk in India new meaning, too.

CHAPTER SEVEN
THE IMPERATIVE OF INNOVATION

> *"Exploration is the engine that drives innovation.*
> *Innovation drives economic growth.*
> *So let's all go exploring."*
>
> — Edith Widder, Oceanographer

People around the world are taking advantage of innovation to drive new ideas and solutions, but the real question is whether you can make these lessons relevant for your business.

Many business theories provide vision that is perfectly clear in hindsight because the theory is enriched by the benefit of history to analyze the elements that made the initiatives successful. The challenge is how to turn these past triumphs into success in the future, particularly when industry dynamics vary so wildly and technology is always on the move.

Additionally, entrepreneurs and small business owners often think that they can't learn from corporate business insights because it is really the capital resources of big business that give large companies their advantage in the marketplace. It is understandable that some would think so; however, a lot of our innovation has come from start-ups, and most start-up companies began on a shoestring. In fact, many of them have grown into powerhouses that dominate their industries from the original vantage point of a garage.

Apple is the company most often cited when pointing out such success stories. In the case of Apple, Steve Jobs didn't even have his *own* garage; he went to his parents' house and asked his father if he could use his garage. Silicon Valley is full of successful ventures that started with just an idea and very little else in terms of resources. These former start-ups, Apple chief among them, are some of the most valuable companies in the world.

All evidence indicates that ideas are really a more vital currency than dollars. The challenge is turning those ideas into meaningful innovation, and that comes by virtue of having the right framework and a good process as your tools. Regardless of your capital resources, these are tools that are at the disposal of businesses of all sizes, at any life stage, and in all industries.

If you are a business owner today and you run a dry cleaners or an interior design firm in an established industry, you might be asking the question of whether innovation is a necessity for you. It may be difficult for you relate to Steve Jobs or even to the young Jennifers who started Rent the Runway. You may have been in business many years, plugging away without any real disruptive change, and this leads you to believe that innovation is not for you.

However, regardless of your industry, innovation is an imperative, and you must go exploring. If you owned a limousine company five years ago, Uber was about to change your business. And if you owned a designer dress shop, Rent the Runway was on your heels, about to break the box of the fashion industry. So who is to say what kind of disrupters are waiting in the wings today to change the business dynamics of your company?

The 3 E's of Innovation are based on principles that stand the test of time, regardless of changes in technology and trends. The real key for utilizing these principles and driving meaningful innovation forward in your business is adopting a process that applies directly to your situation.

The first secret to making this process work is to optimize collaboration between your people and have the discipline to ask the right questions.

People who work on an assembly line, like the one that Henry Ford designed, do the same task over and over and then pass the product along to the next station for the next group. They are not really poised for innovation. Make no mistake, the innovation inherent in the assembly line was a mighty force that rocketed American manufacturing to the forefront as an industrialized nation in its time. It is just not an organizational design that allows teams to collaborate on their most valuable asset—their ideas.

Great innovations happen when organic ideas spring from the collaboration between individuals—not by automatons cranking out parts assembly with precision. Innovative ideas sometimes happen as a result of crisis, such as when frozen turkey becomes a TV dinner. However, you don't want to wait for the crisis to enable your business to innovate. Enablement can come every day by way of a common framework and a consistent process to help align thinking, like the Principle of the 3 E's, and to fuel creativity.

To be successful, these box breakers have to be a team effort, not individual effort. So let's start by looking at talent.

CHAPTER EIGHT

BUILD YOUR TEAM. LET YOUR TEAM BUILD.

> *"Talent wins games. But teamwork wins championships."*
> — *Michael Jordan*

Looking back to some of the great inventions of the past century will give us a clue about the power of teams and why teamwork is mission-critical to any innovation process.

If you stop to think about the greatest breakthroughs of the past century, what inventions would you name? Most people would include Edison's light bulb, Ford's automobile, or the

Wright Brothers' airplane. Of course, many people would say the computer has been the greatest new invention of the past century. There are two important things about these inventions that we need to consider:

1. The people who invented them
2. When they were invented

THE PEOPLE

First of all, none of the great inventions of the past century were the creation of a single individual. Teams of people created them all. And when we think of underutilized assets within our organization, our talent may possibly be the most underutilized of all.

Most often, we like to attribute inventions to a single person, but when we stop and examine the history closely, we find there was a team of people behind it. Thomas Edison had a group of engineers at Menlo Park testing filaments for his light bulbs. Steve Jobs had Steve Wozniak and a group of their friends working in his parents' garage to invent the Apple. The Wright Brothers worked together as a team to man the first successful powered aircraft. Teams of people do great things together. Innovation rarely happens in isolation.

Secondly, none of these inventions of the past century were actually invented for the first time by the people we attribute them to in the list above. We mentioned in an earlier chapter that Karl Benz invented the first commercially produced car, but actually eighty years before him, a French inventor, Francois de Rivaz, built an automobile that was powered by internal combustion. Benz certainly benefited from what de Rivaz created, just as Ford benefited from what Benz created. Each of them innovated on the others' invention. Similarly, Edison did not invent the light bulb; almost 75 years before he filed his patent, an inventor named Humphrey Davy created the "arc lamp" electric-powered light. It was too bright (much like a search light) for commercial use, but it was an electric light bulb, nonetheless.

What about the Wright Brothers? Those were the guys who really invented powered flight back in 1908, right? Well consider this quote that was published in 1909, the year after the Wright Brothers lifted off at Kitty Hawk:

> "About 100 years ago an Englishman, Sir George Cayley, carried the science

of flying to a point which it had never reached before and which it scarcely reached again during the last century."

That might sound like sour grapes written by an inventor who was jealous of the attention the Wrights were getting, but in reality, that is a quote written by Wilber Wright himself. He was acknowledging the work of Cayley, who had designed an aircraft capable of a sustained flight almost a century before—a development that was pivotal to what ultimately spelled success for the Wrights. In each of these cases, it is not individuals who created great things. It was teams of people working together and building on the collective knowledge of those who had gone ahead of them.

This evidence really debunks the theory that changing times and shifting market dynamics make it impossible to learn from the past. On the contrary, the innovation we enjoy today is 100 percent beholden to the inventions and efforts of those who went before us.

THE WHEN

We love to brag about the advancements and the great inventions of the past century, but here is a shocker: nothing much new has really been invented in the past century. That sounds like a bold statement, but examine the dates of the light bulb, the car, and the airplane.

None of these items was created within the past 100 years. *They are all over a century old.*

> The lightbulb—patented by Edison in 1880
> The car—patented by Benz in 1886
> The airplane—flew at Kitty Hawk in 1908

Of course, the computer is not on this list. It has been celebrated as the most impactful of any modern invention. The computer is actually the *oldest* invention on the list.

Charles Babbage invented the programmable computer in 1822. We are approaching two centuries since the invention of the computer. The London Science Museum constructed Babbage's "Difference Engine" in 2002 and proved that his invention from 1822 worked. The golden age of the computer we live in today is not the result of invention but is instead a product of mass adoption fueled by meaningful innovation.

This is not to diminish the fabulous advancements that have been made to the computer in the past century. The computer is now smaller, faster, and more affordable for personal use. The computer that Charles Babbage invented was none of those things. His machine was only capable of rudimentary calculations, and it would have been much too large and too expensive to build for the purposes computers are used for today. For instance, we now carry more computing power in our pocket than the NASA team had at their disposal to solve the Apollo 13 crisis.

These advancements are further evidence that the 3 E's really are key drivers of meaningful innovation. In others words, the computer is more *economical, easy* to use, and ultimately more *ecological* to use today. If you analyze the meaningful innovation in the case of all four of these invention—light bulbs, cars, airplanes, and computers—they are actually just innovations of earlier inventions. They evolved in such a way that the consumer use case for each of them is now *economical, easy,* and *ecological.*

Most importantly, they were the product of collaboration between people, sometimes building on ideas from a century prior. It is a powerful concept. The golden age of technology was ushered in during the 1970s and 1980s in Silicon Valley and has been sustained there because of the collaboration and cross-pollination of innovators. During that time, Hewlett Packard began to bring young technological whiz kids together to share ideas. Steve Jobs, Steve Wozniak, and Bill Gates, along with hundreds of other innovators of the personal computer era, all participated in these collaborative, and sometimes competitive, events. The resulting companies that were born out of that, and even the laptop that I am using today, are shining examples of what happens when collaborative minds come together to create.

How might you bring these principles to life at your company and harness the power of your team to drive meaningful innovation? The answer is a five-step disciplined process that starts with talent and works within the framework of the Principle of the 3 E's.

CHAPTER NINE
STEP TO THE MUSIC

PROCESS STEP ONE:

> *"Come together."*
>
> Lennon and McCartney

What is your company doing to promote cross-functional and truly diverse idea sharing among your employees?

First of all, you must build a culture of collaboration. As organizations grow, they naturally build out groups in functional silos. This is akin to the assembly-line mentality of Henry Ford mentioned earlier. That mentality has indeed facilitated manufacturing, but it is a serial killer of innovation.

Figure out what jobs you want people to do and have them do that, and only that, every day, and you will make absolutely certain that innovation will not happen. Ford revolutionized manufacturing with his theory, but if you are not actively breaking down the walls between departments and people, the strict division of responsibility and lack of communication will completely thwart your progress. This is true regardless of the size of your company or the industry you serve.

Human nature is such that we are attracted to like-minded people. The reality is that like-minded people are not naturally driving toward innovation because thinking alike produces more thinking alike, and they are not prone to out of the box thinking. Like-minded energy drives toward homogony. It's only when we embrace diversity of thought that we can break through to new ideas. Research now validates that organizations with environments where diversity thrives are higher performing companies.

According to Betsy Myers, founding director of the Center for Women and Business at Bentley University, "All of the current research shows that diversity of color, culture, gender—and most importantly, thought—in an organization gives companies a competitive advantage." Myers adds, "What we are hearing from most companies is 'You don't have to convince us that [diversity] is the right thing to do, we just don't know how to do it."

One thing *not to do* is simply hire people of diverse backgrounds and experiences at your company and expect a collaborative culture to emerge. Business cultures must be actively fostered in order to create an environment where associates cross-pollinate ideas with each other. Most people need external stimuli to interact with others who are not like-minded.

However, most of us have participated in company sponsored team building events and then seen short-lived results. Sometimes these activities have the reverse effect, actually causing resentment among the workforce. But companies that truly foster cultures of diversity and actively support efforts that promote opportunities for cross-functional collaboration are building an environment that is ripe for innovation.

One shining example from a company I recently worked with, PSCU in St. Petersburg, Florida, demonstrated how this can be done very creatively through an event called *Rockovate*. The concept was born when two associates who worked in different departments realized they both loved to play acoustic guitar, so they brought their guitars into work one day and stayed late after work for a jam session.

It was fun, but it also brought them together on common ground, which always promotes understanding and collaboration. As others stopped by to hear the music, they joined in the spirit as well. The next day, as those who participated walked down the hall or bumped into each other grabbing coffee, they noticed a difference: a smile, a nod, a knowing glance. Suddenly, there was new commonality and it gave them an idea.

Why not create an event that gets employees to form bands? Any type of music, instruments, and vocals were welcomed; the only rule was that different departments had to be represented. After giving the bands six months to form and practice, they hosted a concert to showcase the bands. The ticket sales benefited one of the company's charities, and the concert was open to friends and families, as well as the community at large.

The idea was met with great enthusiasm, and the employees found a company executive to sponsor the idea and bring it along under the umbrella of their philanthropy efforts. The results were amazing.

When asked about the final result, Lynn Heckler, the Executive Vice President of human resources who attended said of the event, "It was the best example of my career of an event that worked to inspire collaboration, employee engagement, innovation, and diversity and inclusion." On the stage were bands made of technology geeks performing side by side with accounting nerds. As the bands formed and they began to work together, those labels fell away because the bands had joined forces to build their collaboration muscle. They formed a bond that is now strong and long lasting. Heckler added, "These guys conceived a brilliant idea and PSCU reaps the benefits."

ASK THE RIGHT QUESTIONS:

1. Who are you actually hiring (versus who you are interviewing)?
2. What does your "thought diversity" quotient look like?
3. How diverse are the people who most influence decisions for investing your company's money?
4. What have you done to create an environment at your company that actively promotes cross-functional yet organic collaboration?

At the end of the day, it is collaboration that is mission-critical to innovation. One thing does not exist without the other, so take all the time necessary to get this step right.

PROCESS STEP TWO:

> *"Show me whatcha got."*
>
> V.I.C., The Wobble

What is available to you today that is either underutilized or can be actively exploited in a new way?

In the case of Apollo 13, the engineers at NASA were able to quickly assemble the assets that were on board the spacecraft that could be used to build a filter because everything on board was carefully catalogued and the list was at their fingertips. That ability to put their hands on their assets was a vital one for them, but is not often easy for you if haven't thought about it. You must know what you have and give your teams *easy* access to be able to deploy quickly and innovate effectively.

To illustrate, I recently worked with a mid-sized company that provided call center technology and it acquired a smaller company. The reason for the acquisition was because the smaller company had developed a proprietary technology to speed up call time. Solving a customer problem through a call center is always the primary goal, but doing so quickly is the lynchpin for profitability.

As often happens in cases like this acquisition, many of the knowledge workers were laid off once it was complete, and some left on their own. To complicate matters, the larger company did not do a thorough job of assessing either the talent or the underlying technology assets they had acquired as part of the merger, so access to vital information was lost. Several years later, a product was being developed that enabled consumers who called into the center to be automatically enrolled in a special program without having to spend a long time on the phone giving the agent their information.

Rapid enrollment was key to profitability for the company and it also saved time for the consumers who benefited from the new program. So it was vitally important not to have to ask the customer too many questions when they called. However, the technology team found it hard to pull out the specific information they needed from the customer information files to autopopulate the form because those fields had not been consistently codified in the consumers' data files. A manual fix was the only obvious way to retrofit the database, but with many millions of records, it was not economically feasible.

At least that is what they thought. A manager just happened to ask one of the developers who had come over from the little technology company they acquired, and as fate would have it, he actually had coded those fields for a different project years before. The employee was able to quickly deploy his previous work for this project and get it in production quickly. Note that in this example, the result was sheer luck; but you do not want your company to rely on luck when there is a better way.

To make sure you are not missing existing assets that may be hidden or are have not been adequately utilized, you need to add this step to the process with every project or initiative you undertake:

ASK THE RIGHT QUESTIONS:

1. What do you have today that is underutilized? How can you combine that with other assets to create something new?
2. Do you actively poll team members not directly on the project or outside the company to see what they know about possible assets?
3. What insights can past endeavors contribute on available tools and technology to solve your problem?

Just like the Mama Bird that picked up the clump of fur, you might be surprised at the utility of what you find in your backyard that you can use as a box breaker; remember to build in asset lists and create a system that helps the team catalog and easily search in the future.

Check out your supply closet for plenty of duct tape, too.

PROCESS STEP THREE:

> ***"Mo Money. Mo Problems."***
> *The Notorious B.I.G., Mase, and Puff Daddy*

What can you do to make your solution radically economical?

The final use case for any widely adopted innovation must be *economical* if it is going to gain mass acceptance. We saw this with Uber and Rent the Runway. Radical economy is a force for disruption that is happening today with many industries. It is vital that your innovation is affordable or it is not going to change the game.

A great example of this came about as a result of a project that was assigned to two students at Stanford's Hasso Plattner Institute of Design, also known as the "D School." They were paired up with a non-profit organization that needed to find a more affordable option for treating children with clubfoot, a congenital disorder that often leaves patients permanently lame. This is especially true for children born with clubfoot in underserved areas that do not have access to adequate medical care. The traditional treatment sometimes requires surgery and many years of orthopedic braces that could cost thousands of dollars. That is just not a possibility for the majority of children around the world born with this birth defect.

When the two students at Stanford were challenged to design a solution, and they were given a goal of delivering a final product that cost less than $20. The D School gave them access to a great laboratory environment and lots of nifty resources like 3-D printers. Through research of current treatments and strong collaboration, they did it. They devised a colorful injection-molded brace called MiracleFeet that could be easily used in the most remote areas around the world. Their brace now makes it possible for patients to stand up and play on their own. Interestingly, because of the way it is made, it doesn't look like a medical device at all. Many people mistake the MiracleFeet device for a new toy. Happily, the solution is now in full production and being shipped to children all over the world.

This type of innovation could have actually been possible years before; the model for the MiracleFeet brace is actually an innovation on an orthopedic device that has been on the market for many years. However, the original device was made of heavy metal and was very expensive. The students at Stanford did not invent a totally new product, they brought meaningful innovation with extreme economy to one that already existed.

Imagine for a minute what response the non-profit organization would have received if they approached the original medical device manufacturer for a more affordable option. Executives would likely have offered to donate a small portion of these devices as a philanthropic gesture. The company might have even put a team on the project to iterate a somewhat less expensive device. Could you imagine that they would invent a device that cost less than $20 when they had been charging hundreds? The mandates of any company created to generate profits would prevent them from creating something as affordable as MiracleFeet - radically compression of profit margins is not the kind of box breaker most companies are looking for, to say the least.

The device exists today because the students at Stanford were actually challenged to do the opposite—to make it as inexpensively as possible. As a result, the MiracleFeet device is quickly replacing the metal device that inspired it, not just in poor and undeveloped countries, but everywhere. The plastic device works just as well as the expensive metal device. The solution created for the very poor children in the undeveloped countries is also the perfect solution for families who can afford anything they want. The lighter weight of the plastic is more effective for young children, and the possibility of endless bright colors makes the brace more fun for them to wear.

Just as Diane von Furstenberg was not the place to create the Rent the Runway concept, the medical device company was probably not the place to take the clubfoot brace innovation. The lesson here is obvious: innovation is going to happen in your industry. If you are not looking at radically *economical* ways to solve problems at your company with the same attitude someone from outside your company would approach them, then sooner or later you will be disrupted.

> **ASK THE RIGHT QUESTIONS:**
>
> 1. If your competitor wanted to put you out of business, at what price would they market your product or service?
> 2. How much would someone who knows nothing about your business expect to pay for your product?
> 3. If profit were no longer a consideration for you, what price would you set for your products?

If you can't make your solution radically *economical*, then your competitors, or disruptors from outside your industry, certainly will.

PROCESS STEP FOUR:

> *"Because I'm easy.*
> *Easy like Sunday morning."*
>
> Lionel Richie

Are you actively finding solutions that are easy for the ultimate user?

It is very hard to make things easy, and it is not simple to keep them from becoming complex. But at the end of the day, if solutions are not *easy*, then they are not likely to be widely adopted. Even products that solve problems or provide great benefit will not be successful if they aren't easy.

Adoption means that products have to be used by people with varying degrees of intelligence and aptitude. A design engineer may think his or her product is *easy*, but that engineer is probably too blinded by their education, experience, and personal paradigms to relate to the consumer who needs the product. Engineers are mighty smart, but it is human nature that prevents them from "unknowing" what they know in order to look at product design objectively. However, when testing is done directly with the end user and the result is truly *easy* for them, then the solution can meet with raging success.

As a personal example of this, several years ago, my oldest daughter moved into her first apartment. Since she was just starting out, she had a very limited budget, but she also needed absolutely everything—from furniture to dishes. Luckily she had done her research and suggested we visit IKEA to maximize her budget and get the majority of what we needed in one location. If you are not familiar with IKEA, it is the world's largest furniture retailer, specializing in low-cost designs that have broad appeal for the Millennial Generation.

So off we went to IKEA, and my daughter had indeed done her homework. She had the list of furniture, kitchenware, and accessories picked out from the website in hand. As a result, we blew through the IKEA store in an hour. She took pictures of the tags with her phone, and our checkout was a breeze. Since we didn't own a truck, she had also arranged for a delivery service to bring the items to her apartment. However, it was not until they delivered the goods to us the next day that I realized we had gotten ourselves into a pickle with this purchase. The delivery crew brought in box after huge box and set them in her living room until they became a veritable mountain range. Last, but by no means least, they carried in a large box containing parts for a very heavy sleeper sofa.

 When I realized that "assembly required" was going to be the operative phrase for the next two days, I begged the deliveryman to stay and help us put the furniture together. He was adamant that they only delivered; they did not assemble. When he saw the fear and dread spread over my face, he assured me, "It's really easy, Ma'am. Even you girls can do it." I believe he was chuckling on the way out the door. Of course, when he said "even you girls," we became determined to get it done.

 We actually did prove that he was right, because two days later, we had assembled a bed, a dresser, a kitchen table, four bar stools, two end tables, a coffee table, and yes, a sleeper sofa. We followed the instructions included in that mountain range of boxes, and the only tools we needed to use were a couple of screwdrivers. As we stepped back and took a moment of justifiable pride to gaze over our momentous accomplishment, I was extremely thankful for the engineers at IKEA. But I also realized they must do an enormous amount of user testing to make it that *easy*. It is likely the very reason that the company is the largest furniture retailer in the world. They broke the box by making it easy!

> **ASK THE RIGHT QUESTIONS:**
>
> 1. Are the complexities of your solution necessary or is that just the way it has always been done?
> 2. If you could answer the question "Wouldn't it be awesome if …," how might your solution work?
> 3. What would a person totally unfamiliar with your solution or product say about how *easy/hard* it is?

With so many distractions today, consumers are constantly looking for solutions to save time, so creating solutions that are *easy* is key. Breaking your box by truly analyzing whether your new product or service is easier to use by asking the end user will be the differentiator that spells success.

PROCESS STEP FIVE:

> *"In dreams we do so many things*
> *We set aside the rules we know*
> *And fly the world so high*
> *In great and shining rings."*
>
> Roy Orbison, In the Real World

To be successful you need to create your innovation by setting aside the rules you know. To drive meaningful innovation that will achieve mass adoption, you have to also see how your product or solution works in the real world. Thorough testing is required to gain this knowledge. Getting user feedback from people inside, but mostly *outside*, of your company (and especially outside of your industry) is mission critical to ensure the concept's success.

Very often, companies are solving for a problem that people don't have, and innovation for the sake of innovation will not meet with mass adoption.

As we established previously, innovation must solve a problem or meet a perceived need to be meaningful.

A great example of how *not* to do this has been examined endlessly by business analysts. It was the introduction of "New Coke" back in 1985. I had the opportunity to see this drama up close. I worked for a company that did a lot of commercial printing for The Coca-Cola Company in Atlanta, and I remember distinctly the events surrounding the announcement of the new product.

At the time, I was in sales and had Lockheed Aircraft as a client. The company I worked for printed marketing materials to promote their planes. Some of those projects were sensitive, although never classified, but we took extra care when we were working for Lockheed to keep the information on a need-to-know basis.

The owner of my company called me into his office one day and asked me if I had any projects coming up for Lockheed. He suggested mysteriously that if I could bring one in, he would be willing to produce it for a greatly discounted price. The stipulation was that I must bring the project in within the next two days. I suffered a bit with my own curiosity, but I managed to secure one of those projects.

As soon as I got back with it, he shut the printing plant down for everything except printing the Lockheed project and, unbeknownst to me, also the marketing materials for New Coke. His strategy was brilliant, because all of the employees working in the printing plant thought that the security guards he stationed at the doors were to protect the Lockheed project. No one noticed the banner on the Coke posters that said "New." The product announcement was hidden in plain sight. His plan also worked because nobody could conceive of Coke ever changing. It was a sacred brand.

Of course, for that reason, just three months later, we were printing massive amounts of advertising materials that announced the return of "Coke Classic." Consumers were enraged that The Coca-Cola Company would change the formula of their beloved soft drink. And they demanded that it be returned to them—immediately!

Luckily for the company, Coke was able to recover from its mistake because people were passionate about the product. In fact, the loyalty to the original formula was so deeply rooted in the Coke brand that it is still being analyzed and marveled at 30 years later.

In June of 1985, at the press conference announcing that The Coca-Cola Company was bringing the original formula back, Donald Keough, the company president, said, "All of the time and money and skill that we poured into consumer research could not reveal the depth of feeling for the original taste of Coca-Cola. Some cynics say we planned the whole thing as a marketing ploy to drive up sales. The truth is we are not that dumb and we are not that smart."

The mistake The Coca-Cola Company made was one that many other businesses make all the time, just without the benefit of a century of brand loyalty to act as a net for their high-wire act. The company solved a problem people didn't have to begin with—people liked the taste of Coke just as it was.

Good business processes can keep your company from making the same mistake as New Coke. As Roy Orbison once sang in the song "The Real World," we should "Fly the world so high," but we should also come back down to earth safely. Because without extraordinarily rare customer loyalty like Coke had to support your efforts, the fall can prove to be fatal for your business.

In a more recent example, we can take a look at the debacle of Google Glass. With great expense and much fanfare, Google launched its latest innovation in wearable computers for the high price of $1,500 per pair. The product was then pulled off the market shortly after its launch.

Here is at least part of the reason: most people who do not wear glasses today are not yearning to find a way to wear them. Glasses are mostly an inconvenience, even to people who need them to be able to see. Which is why people get contacts and undergo Lasik eye surgery. The practical, down-to-earth truth is this: if you don't wear glasses, you really don't want to wear glasses. So by choosing this format for their wearable computer, Google was not meeting a perceived need or solving a problem. In fact, if you already wore glasses, you couldn't wear Google Glass.

An additional major issue for Google was that they forgot to tell people that the product was not ready for prime time. The negative sentiment came on especially strong from consumers who value their privacy, since they were not informed that the glasses were gathering information from them. Everything they did, every place they went, and everything they saw was information Google collected. This feature evoked shades of George Orwell's *1984* and was very bad for Google's brand. No company wants to be compared to "Big Brother." And no consumer wants to be the owner of a very expensive pair of glasses at the expense of giving up privacy. The backlash against Google has been strong and its investment in this product now amounts to a massive loss.

Additionally, Google promoted the product to its corporate partnerships as being market ready, and many of those companies began investing their own millions to create supporting products for Google Glass. That mistake has seriously hurt Google's credibility in an area that is vital to future business success. Disenfranchising your business partners is never a good idea.

If Google had taken its time to thoroughly test the use case for the Google Glass product, the company's time and money would have been better spent. Wearable technology is the wave of the future, and down the road, some meaningful innovation that truly solves a problem will appear. Apple Watch could potentially be that innovation; people continued to wear watches in spite of the fact that they became a "single function device." This indicates that making the wearable computer in the form of the watch instead of glasses has a higher potential for success. But box breakers only work when innovators like Apple follow through with a process of disciplined inside-out testing.

ASK THE RIGHT QUESTIONS:

1. What market force motivated you to create this solution? How much will people have to change to adopt your idea?
2. What problem will it solve for your customers today? What about customers tomorrow?
3. What is the perceived need that will cause this solution to reach mass adoption for your ultimate user?

Take the time to analyze the perceived need on the part of your market and really focus on the problems your solution is addressing. Have the courage to go back to the drawing board if your honest answers to these questions lead you to the conclusion that your product is not ready for prime time." Take the time and spend the money necessary to make sure before you launch that customers will want to pick up what you are putting down.

CONCLUSION

Ideas are the most vital currency of a company, an industry, a country, or a culture. Ideas drive innovation, and without continual innovation the advancements of yesterday can quickly become the boat anchor of success for tomorrow. Finding those ideas that are truly the box breakers is the secret to success.

As business people, we are wise to learn the lessons of those who have gone before us, like the team in Houston that brought the Apollo 13 astronauts home. Those who have experienced success can teach us, and we can learn from the efforts of those who have failed as well. The bottom line is this: with a good business process that supports a culture of collaboration and the discipline to ask the right questions of our people and those outside our company, we can increase the likelihood of success for our future efforts.

Taking advantage of the Principle of the 3 E's is one way to get there. Make sure your ideas are *easy* for users, radically *economical,* and most important of all, *ecological.* Dump everything you have on the table, metaphorically, and catalog all of your assets as the starting point.

Look for underutilized assets because the business ecosystem will eventually solve for the waste if you do not. It is empowering to understand that is subject to the same dynamic that drives the natural ecosystem. So be constantly mindful of excess in your business, both the tangible assets and the more intangible ones of human talent. When you find anything underutilized consider it a canary in your coalmine.

The Book of Ecclesiastes says, "There is no new thing under the sun." This does not mean that there is nothing innovative under the sun, because there is plenty. And it is all at our fingertips if we can bring our teams together, access the insights from what has been done before, and take advantage of our assets and talents to create innovations to improve our lives and ultimately improve our world.

It's all about willingness to break the box.

POST SCRIPT
STREET CRED

I have been fortunate to work for some truly great companies, and I have learned a lot from being exposed to amazing clients who have been innovators in their industries, such as The Coca-Cola Company, MasterCard, and the International Olympic Committee.

I have been able to gain valuable insight into the innovation process through roles inside some of these companies as an employee, along with my perspective in consulting roles with many great companies. Those experiences gave me the opportunity to create a conceptual framework that I now use to help clients in many different industries access innovation in unique and more meaningful ways.

One recent opportunity to use this framework came along quite serendipitously.

I joined a company as executive vice president with strong encouragement from its new CEO, who recruited me to infuse the company culture with more creativity. My early suggestion to him was that we create a place on the office campus that was dedicated to innovation—a lab of sorts. This would help us reframe the way our company's associates, clients, and vendor partners approached meetings and provide them with an environment more intentionally designed to facilitate creative collaboration.

The new CEO was supportive, so I got an estimate from a contractor to build an innovation lab and the bill was going to be hefty. Additionally, our office space on campus was already crowded and it was counterintuitive to ask associates to give up their space to work from home in order to build a lab to enhance their collaboration!

After working late one day, I walked around the office campus, pondering the dilemma, and just happened upon some office space that had been vacated by the previous CEO. His empty office looked out on a lake with floor-to-ceiling windows and there was a smaller office space in the ante area that had been used by his administrative assistant. Wandering through the space, I found his conference room, a small kitchen, and a restroom adjacent to his office.

This space had not been utilized for other offices because the layout was not really appropriate, so it sat vacant for over a year after the unexpected death of the previous CEO. Additionally, the employees so dearly loved this man that no one had the heart to suggest using his office for anything else.

As I looked through the rooms, I saw how we could take out a few walls and open up the space for the innovation lab. The kitchen area and restroom were actually an added bonus because we would need both functions to support any all-day meetings we wanted to have there. Those floor-to-ceiling windows drew in the natural light and view of the serene lake would only enhance the creative energy flow we were trying to encourage. It had everything we needed to help our employees "break the box."

When I checked with the contractor, he suggested we paint all of the walls with whiteboard paint and bring in modular furniture. The tables and chairs could be made on wheels to allow meetings to break up into small groups and then come back together.

Altogether, the cost for creating this space was a fraction of the previous estimate—and it was accomplished by using what we already had in a new way. It was a quick fix and the innovation lab soon became a magnet for associates and customers to come together to brainstorm new ideas.

It was *easy, ecological,* and *economical.*

As a final note, Dave Serlo, the man who founded the company was an innovator in his own right. He created a concept for his industry that had never been tried before, and he courageously led his company through over twenty years of successful growth before his untimely death. He left a legacy impacting thousands of people and positively affecting their careers, lives, and families.

So, it may have been serendipity that brought me to his old office that day. And it may have been the framework of the Principle of the 3 E's that gave me insight to build the innovation lab.

Or it may just have been Dave.

ACKNOWLEDGEMENTS

I've learned that it takes a village to write a book. So I want to acknowledge the people who inspired me and helped with this effort. This is not a comprehensive list, but some of them I absolutely have to mention by name.

Ashley Oliphant, an English professor at Pfeiffer University in North Carolina and a published author, served as my first unofficial editor before Howard, Cyndy, and the team at Paradies Publishing took the reins. She spent many hours with critiques early in the process, which made the book a much better product. She also happens to be my niece, and she was raised by one strong and amazing woman, my sister Beth Yarbrough, who publishes *Southern Voice* and always inspires me.

Tom Beatty, a long time business colleague and now a treasured friend, told me that I had to write a book. He didn't really offer up another option the day I took him to breakfast to tell him I was starting a new business as a consultant. He just said I had to write a book. So I started it that day.

My good friend and playwright, Melita Easters, inspired me with her creativity and constant encouragement. Angela Rey, a marketing genius at the Tampa agency, Energyhill, both pushed and pulled me to make this book a reality. James Green, who was a former business colleague and is always an instigator of innovation, read it thoroughly and provided honest and practical feedback.

Dr. Arvind Deogirikir, a technology guru and mentor to many people, guided me through his home country of India and helped to open my mind while encouraging my spirit. Michael Dinkins, my business mentor, took me under his wing twenty years ago and has never given up on me since, quite remarkably.

My San Francisco daughter, Angie McDonald, an art director extraordinaire, along with her amazing group of imaginative friends in the heart of all things cool, constantly supported me in the notion that I had ideas worth sharing. And my Atlanta daughter, Katy Young, was always there with her business insights, which are substanitive. I am blessed to have two such incredible and talented girls and such a rich network of bright and supportive colleagues and friends.

So many thanks.

BONUS OFFER FOR READERS OF THIS BOOK:

Download a free workbook that shows you how to utilize the innovation process at your company. Visit http://fredda.leadpages.co/workbook/

ABOUT THE AUTHOR

Fredda McDonald's career has been characterized by measurable business results in a variety of senior executive roles in both corporations and as an entrepreneur. She has had success in consulting services, sales and account management, marketing, and branding. Most recently, she formed a new consulting company called Lydian Management Consulting. She took the name as tribute to the innovative people of the sixth century BC who changed commerce forever by inventing the first coin, called the Lydia.

Immediately prior to starting her own firm, McDonald served as executive vice president of PSCU—the nation's largest credit union services organization—where her leadership was instrumental in driving innovation and successfully navigating the company through the most rapid growth and change in its 30-year history. The team she led was able to positively impact revenue at the same time awareness was created for the company's distinctly new brand. Most notably, the programs she developed also raised awareness and membership in credit unions nationally.

From 2005 – 2011 at MasterCard Worldwide, McDonald led the team that oversaw relationships with financial technology giants FIS, Fiserv, TSYS, and First Data. She developed innovative strategies to partner with these clients for mutual success.

Lydian Management is not the first entrepreneurial endeavor for McDonald. She had her own consulting firm, Mentor Management Group, that worked with high-tech startups and companies, large and small, that were experiencing radical changes in the late 1990s and early 2000s. She had the honor to be tapped by Meridian Management to facilitate the global brand plan of the International Olympic Committee based in Lausanne, Switzerland. This allowed her to interface at a strategic level with the major corporations that sponsor the IOC, such as Visa and Coca-Cola.

Previous to that, she was CEO of Cadmus Marketing Services—a company that served many of those same major brands as clients.

In addition to her accomplishments as an executive, McDonald is a highly sought-after speaker and regular contributor to many business publications. She was recently awarded the prestigious WOCCU bronze medal in 2014 in Australia for her presentation at the annual meeting of the World Council of Credit Unions.

Her interests outside of the professional realm include travel, history, cooking, and fiction writing. She has two grown daughters; one lives in Atlanta and the other in San Francisco. Regular visits to the Bay Area to visit her youngest allow McDonald to be enveloped in an intensely innovative business culture and also provide her daughter and friends with an opportunity to eat her Southern home cooking.

Contact:
Fredda McDonald
LYDIAN Management Consulting
fredda@lydianmgt.com
912-223-3859

REFERENCES

Apollo 13. DVD. Directed by Ron Howard. 1995: Universal City, CA: Universal Studios Home Entertainment, 1996.

"Aarambh Help Desk for Children," *Ureka*, accessed July 2, 2015, http://ureka.my/aarambh-help-desk-children.

Atkinson, Nancy. "13 Things That Saved Apollo 13, Part 10: Duct Tape." *Universe Today*, 26 April 2010. Accessed July 12, 2015. http://www.universetoday.com/63673/13-things-that-saved-apollo-13-part-10-duct-tape.

Bill Gates. BrainyQuote.com, Xplore Inc, 2015. http://www.brainyquote.com/quotes/quotes/b/billgates626215.html, accessed August 10, 2015

Benz, Karl. DRP's Patent No. 37435 filed January 28, 1886, accessed August 10, 2015. https://en.wikipedia.org/wiki/Karl_Benz.

Duke Ellington. BrainyQuote.com. Xplore Inc, 2015. http://www.brainyquote.com/quotes/quotes/d/dukeelling103831.html, accessed August 10, 2015.

"Ecology." *Merriam-Webster.com*. 2015, accessed July 11, 2015. http://www.merriam-webster.com/dictionary/ecology.

Galilei Galileo. BrainyQuote.com Xplore, Inc. 2015. http://www.brainyquote.com/quotes/quotes/g/galileogal381318.html, accessed August 10, 2015.

"Gender Intelligence: The Competitive Advantage of Gender Intelligence." *Center for Women & Business – Bentley University*, accessed July 14, 2015, http://www.bentley.edu/centers/center-for-women-and-business/gender-intelligence-0.

Henry Ford. BrainyQuote.com. Xplore Inc, http://www.brainyquote.com/quotes/quotes/h/henryford122817.html, accessed August 10, 2015.

Heckler, Lynn. Personal interview. 10 August 2015.

Hewlett, Sylvia Ann, Melinda Marshall, and Laura Sherbin. "How Diversity Can Drive Innovation." *Harvard Business Review*, December 2013, accessed July 15, 2015, https://hbr.org/2013/12/how-diversity-can-drive-innovation.

"India's One-Man Band." *The Economist*, May 23, 2015, accessed July 15, 2015, http://www.economist.com/news/leaders/21651813-country-has-golden-opportunity-transform-itself-narendra-modi-risks-missing-it-indias.

Isaacson, Walter. *Steve Jobs*. New York: Simon and Schuster, 2011.

Kelly, Rob. "Segway. Hits and Misses." CNN Money. 2007, accessed August 10, 2015, http://money.cnn.com/galleries/2007/biz2/0706/gallery.launch_hits_and_misses.biz2/9.html.

Klara, Robert. "How Swanson's TV Dinners Made It to the Digital Age: Thank American Airlines, 260 tons of turkey and dudes who still can't cook." *Adweek*, April 21, 2015, accessed July 1, 2015, http://www.adweek.com/news/advertising-branding/how-swanson-s-tv-dinners-made-it-digital-age-164127.

Leibling and Bates. "Spaced Out" RAC Foundation. July 2012.

John Lennon, and Paul McCartney, "Come Together," by John Lennon and Paul McCartney, In *Abbey Road*, Capital Records, CD, 2009.

Loeb, Walter. "IKEA." Forbes. 5 December, 2012, accessed August 10, 2015, http://www.forbes.com/sites/walterloeb/2012/12/05/ikea-is-a-world-wide-wonder.

Linn, James J.; "A General Asset Theory." Alfred P. Sloan School of Management, MIT, June 23, 1966, accessed August 10, 2015, http://archive.org/stream/generalassettheo00linn/generalassettheo00linn_djvu.txt

Mamiit, Aaron. "Google Glass is Dead...For Now." *Tech Times*, January 21, 2015, accessed July 15, 2015, http://www.techtimes.com/articles/27759/20150121/google-glass-is-dead-for-now.htm.

Michael Jordan. BrainyQuote.com. XPlore Inc. 2015. http://www.brainyquote.com/quotes/quotes/m/michaeljor167383.html, accessed August 10, 2015.

"Miraclefeet Brace." *Stanford University*, 2012, accessed July 15, 2015, http://extreme.stanford.edu/projects/miraclefeet-brace.

Notorious B.I.G., Sean "Puff Daddy" Combs, B.H. Edwards, S. Jordan, Nile Rodgers, and Mase, "Mo Money Mo Problems," by Notorious B.I.G., Sean "Puff Daddy" Combs, B.H. Edwards, S. Jordan, Nile Rodgers, and Mase, In *Mo Money Mo Problems*, Bad Boy Entertainment, CD, 1997

Richard Kerr and Will Jennings, "In the Real World." Roy Orbison, Virgin, CD, 1989.

Orwell, George. *1984*. New York: Signet, 1961.

Riha, Daniel. "Geek Tech: Apollo Guidance Computer vs. iPhone 5s." *The Daily Crate*, February 1, 2014, accessed July 14, 2015, http://www.thedailycrate.com/2014/02/01/geek-tech-apollo-guidance-computer-vs-iphone-5s.

Lionel Richie. "Easy," by Lionel Richie, in *Commodores*, Motown, CD, 1977.

Saylor, Michael. M-Pesa. *The Mobile Wave: How Mobile Intelligence Will Change Everything*. New York: Vanguard Press, 2012.

Strom, Stephanie. "Donald R. Keough, Who Led Coca-Cola Through New Coke Debacle, Dies at 88." *The New York Times* February 24, 2015, accessed February 24, 2015, http://www.

nytimes.com/2015/02/25/business/donald-r-keough-who-led-coca-cola-through-new-coke-debacle-dies-at-88.html?_r=0.

Swade, Doron. "The Babbage Engine." *Computer History Museum*, 2008, accessed July 14, 2015. http://www.computerhistory.org/babbage/2008,

Adora Svitak." BrainyQuote.com. Xplore Inc, 2015. http://www.brainyquote.com/quotes/quotes/a/adorasvita594723.html, accessed August 10, 2015.

"Thomas Edison and Menlo Park." *The Thomas Edison Center at Menlo Park*. 2009, accessed July 15, 2015, http://www.menloparkmuseum.org/history/thomas-edison-and-menlo-park.

Uber, "Newroom," accessed August 10, 2015, http://newsroom.uber.com.

V.I.C., *Wobble,* V.I.C., Warner Bros, CD, 2008.

Widder, Edith. "Edith Widder." Brainy Quote.com. Xplore Inc. 2015. http://www.brainyquote.com/quotes/quotes/e/edithwidde550187.html, accessed August 10, 2015.

Made in the USA
Charleston, SC
11 October 2015